ACTIVITIES FOR MINECRAFTERS: DUNGEONS

Puzzles and Games for Hours of Fun!

JEN FUNK WEBER

ILLUSTRATED BY
GRACE SANDFORD AND AMANDA BRACK

SKY PONY PRESS
NEW YORK, NEW YORK

Copyright © 2021 by Hollan Publishing, Inc.

Minecraft® is a registered trademark of Notch Development AB.

The Minecraft game is copyright © Mojang AB.

All rights reserved. No part of this book may be reproduced in any manner without the express written consent of the publisher, except in the case of brief excerpts in critical reviews or articles. All inquiries should be addressed to Sky Pony Press, 307 West 36th Street, 11th Floor, New York, NY 10018.

Sky Pony Press books may be purchased in bulk at special discounts for sales promotion, corporate gifts, fund-raising, or educational purposes. Special editions can also be created to specifications. For details, contact the Special Sales Department, Sky Pony Press, 307 West 36th Street, 11th Floor, New York, NY 10018 or info@skyhorsepublishing.com.

Sky Pony® is a registered trademark of Skyhorse Publishing, Inc.®, a Delaware corporation.

Minecraft® is a registered trademark of Notch Development AB.

The Minecraft game is copyright © Mojang AB.

Visit our website at www.skyponypress.com.

10 9 8 7 6 5 4 3 2 1

Library of Congress Cataloging-in-Publication Data is available on file.

Print ISBN: 978-1-5107-6502-3

Cover and interior art by Grace Sandford and Amanda Brack
Additional illustrations used under license from Shutterstock.com

Printed in China

TABLE OF CONTENTS

THE HIDDEN CATACOMB

This wacky map marks the way to a secret Minecraft Dungeon catacomb behind Door A, Door B, or Door C. Follow the arrows until your path leads straight through the secret door (passing by a door doesn't count!).

Begin in the red square. Move in the direction an arrow points until you come to a new arrow. If there are two arrows in a square, you can choose to go either direction.

LOST VILLAGER

A dungeon villager is lost. The word **villager** appears only once in the word search below. It can be forward or backward, in a horizontal, vertical, or diagonal line. Find the word to complete your mission and rescue the villager.

```
V V E G A L L I V G
G I I E V R G I I E
R L L I I L G L R
E L A L L L R E I
V I L L A E R E G L
L G V G L G G G G L
L E E I L A E A E A
I R V I L L V L R G
V I L L A G I I V E
R V I L L A G V E R
```

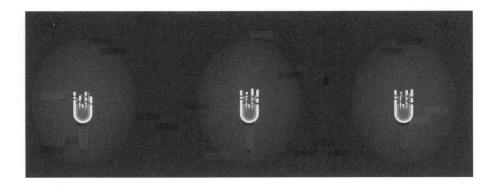

A HEALTHY DOSE OF ADVICE

Completing missions in Minecraft Dungeons requires stamina. This tip will help you maximize your staying power.

Start at the ↓. *Write every third letter on the spaces until they have all been used. If you place them correctly, you'll reveal a tip to chew on.*

K ___ ____ ___ _____ ___

_____ _____.

UNLOCK THE RUNE

One of these 9 buttons is magic. If you press it first, you will touch each button only once, finish on F (final), and unlock the rune to take with you on your journey. You must follow the direction codes on the buttons.

For instance, 2D means press the button two spaces down. R = right. L = left. U = up.

Circle the magic button.

TIP: Collecting 10 runes in Minecraft Dungeons helps you unlock a secret level!

HIDDEN ACRONYM

Match each puzzle piece to its correct spot on the grid (piece A-1 belongs in row A, column 1), and shade the grid squares to match. When you're finished, you'll reveal the name of a gaming term for temporarily leaving the game.

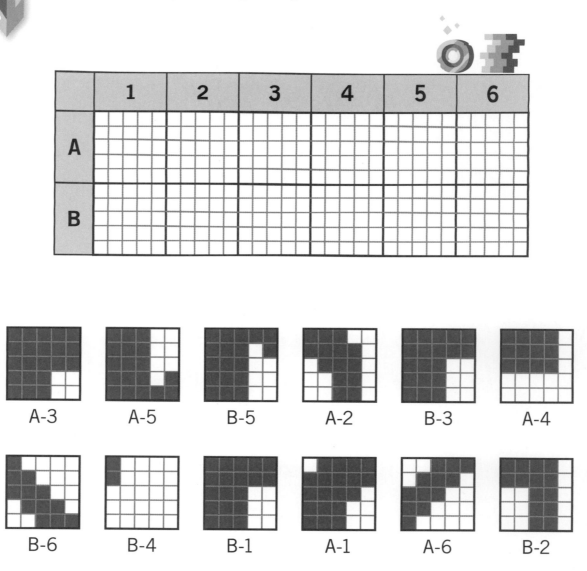

	1	2	3	4	5	6
A						
B						

A-3   A-5   B-5   A-2   B-3   A-4

B-6   B-4   B-1   A-1   A-6   B-2

BATTLE BREAKS

Read the writing on the wall by placing the 2x2 letter blocks in their proper places. If you place them correctly, you'll reveal a Minecraft Dungeons tip worth its weight in . . . well, emeralds.

Heads up: Words are separated by purple squares and wrap from one line to the next.

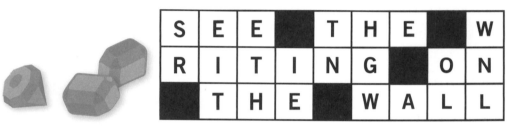

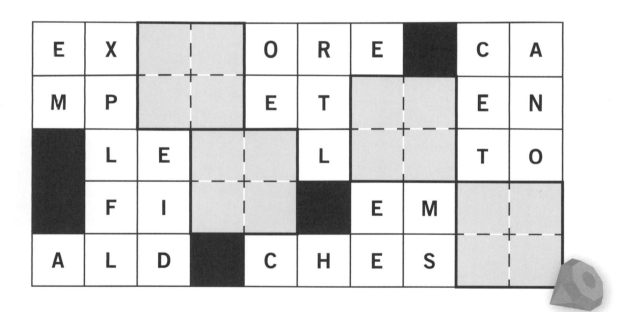

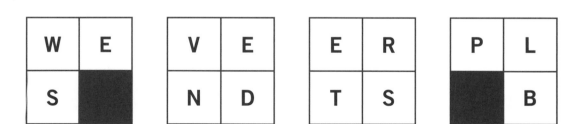

ON THE TRACK OF THE ARTIFACT

Do you know where you can get the five artifacts shown below?

To find out, begin at the dot below each artifact name and follow it downward. Every time you hit a horizontal line (one that goes across), you must take it. Write the name of each artifact below the proper location.

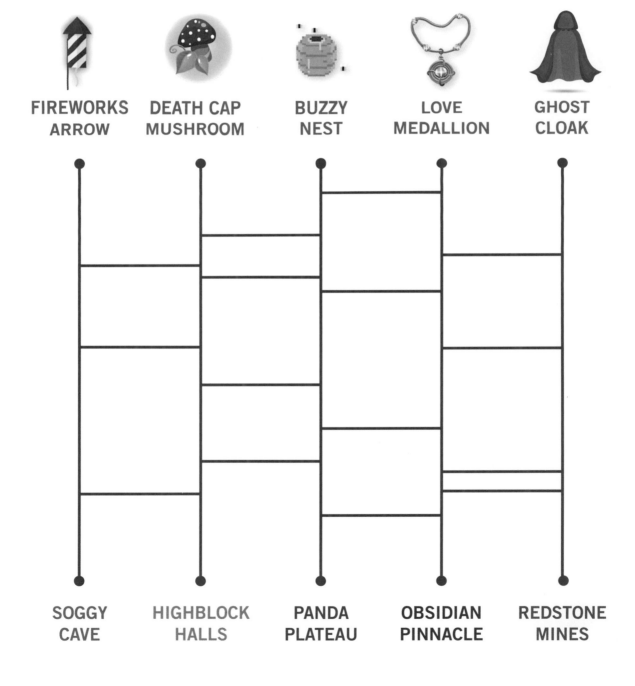

FIREWORKS ARROW   DEATH CAP MUSHROOM   BUZZY NEST   LOVE MEDALLION   GHOST CLOAK

SOGGY CAVE   HIGHBLOCK HALLS   PANDA PLATEAU   OBSIDIAN PINNACLE   REDSTONE MINES

_____ _____ _____ _____ _____

CROSSBOW QUEST

Ranged weapons in Minecraft Dungeons include many different crossbows. Can you find nineteen different crossbows in the letters below? If you find them all, the remaining letters reveal a handy fact about them.

Hint: Circle individual letters instead of whole words so you can see the leftover letters more easily.

Ⓢ Ⓟ Ⓔ Ⓛ Ⓛ Ⓑ Ⓞ Ⓤ Ⓝ Ⓓ H

S	R	H	O	T	T	A	S	F	E	R
O	A	E	M	C	S	R	B	A	T	O
B	H	S	T	S	B	R	V	Y	P	O
U	G	W	S	N	A	Y	U	R	U	R
T	N	C	P	U	A	A	B	R	E
T	I	N	I	N	T	H	D	S	R	T
E	N	D	O	D	O	O	L	O	O	T
R	T	T	B	E	O	A	C	U	C	A
F	H	H	A	M	U	L	R	L	O	C
L	G	N	I	D	O	L	P	M	I	S
Y	I	S	L	A	Y	E	R	X	G	E
D	L	L	U	O	S	L	A	R	E	F

AUTO
BABY
BUTTERFLY
BURST
CORRUPTED
DOOM
DUAL
EXPLODING
FERAL SOUL
HARP
HEAVY
IMPLODING
LIGHTNING
HARP
RAPID
SCATTER
SLAYER
SOUL
SOUL HUNTER
~~SPELLBOUND~~

Unused letters:

__ __ __ __ __   __ __ __ __   __ __ __ __ __ __ __ __ __ __ __

__ __ __ __ __ __ __   __ __ __ __   __ __ __ __ __ __ __ __ .

A FANTASTIC FIND

Every word in Column B contains the same letters as a word in Column A, plus one letter. Draw a line between each word in Column A and its partner in Column B, then write the extra letter on the space provided. Read the column of letters downward to reveal an artifact you might find in the Dingy Jungle. The first one has been done for you.

COLUMN A	COLUMN B	
Tonic	Target	_T_
Nomad	Action	__
Cache	Spider	__
Ocean	Battle	__
Grand	Dynamo	__
Great	Beacon	__
Table	Option	__
Point	Chance	__
Pride	Ranged	__

__ __ __ __ __   __ __ __ __

ARMORED AND DANGEROUS

Each player below is wearing different armor. Read the clues to figure out which player is wearing which kind of armor. Put an X in a box if it can be ruled out. (PopSizzle11 does not have Highland Armor.) Put an O in boxes that are a match.

	ARMOR		
PLAYER	Beenest Armor	Highland Armor	Ember Robe
TagURit			
PopSizzle11		X	
Coool28			

1. TagURit has either Beenest Armor or Highland Armor.

2. PopSizzle11 does not have Highland Armor. It is already X'd out.

3. Coool28 has the one kind of armor not mentioned in clue #1.

ARCH-ILLAGER MAZE

Find your way through the maze to destroy the final boss, the dreaded Arch-illager.

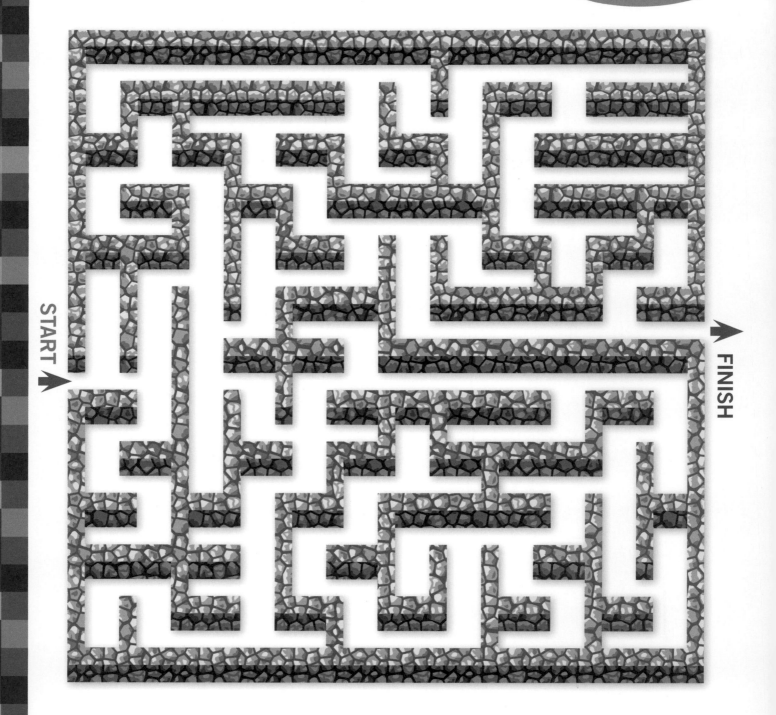

START

FINISH

FIND LOOT

Turn FIND into LOOT one letter at a time. The answer to each clue looks like the word above it, except one letter is different. If you get stuck, try working from the bottom up.

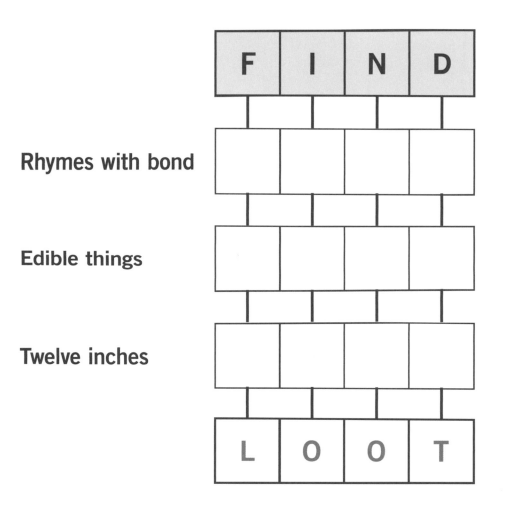

	F	I	N	D

Rhymes with bond

Edible things

Twelve inches

L	O	O	T

A STRING OF MOBS

Put your pencil point on the circled letter in the lower left corner of the grid. Without picking up the point, connect all the letters in the grid vertically or horizontally (not diagonally) to spell the names of five illagers.

Hint: The illager names are listed below in random order.

Example:

T	A	H	Ⓢ
E	B	E	E
E	M	A	P
B	A	L	L

SHEEP
LLAMA
BEE
BAT

C	E	A	L	L	I	P
N	R	G	E	R	E	R
A	M	O	E	G	K	O
C	H	A	N	T	E	V
N	O	R	R	E	D	R
Ⓔ	Y	A	L	G	U	A

EVOKER

PILLAGER

ENCHANTER

ROYAL GUARD

GEOMANCER

SOGGY SWAMP MAZE

This Soggy Swamp Maze is packed with treasure! Can you collect it all on your way from START to FINISH?

START

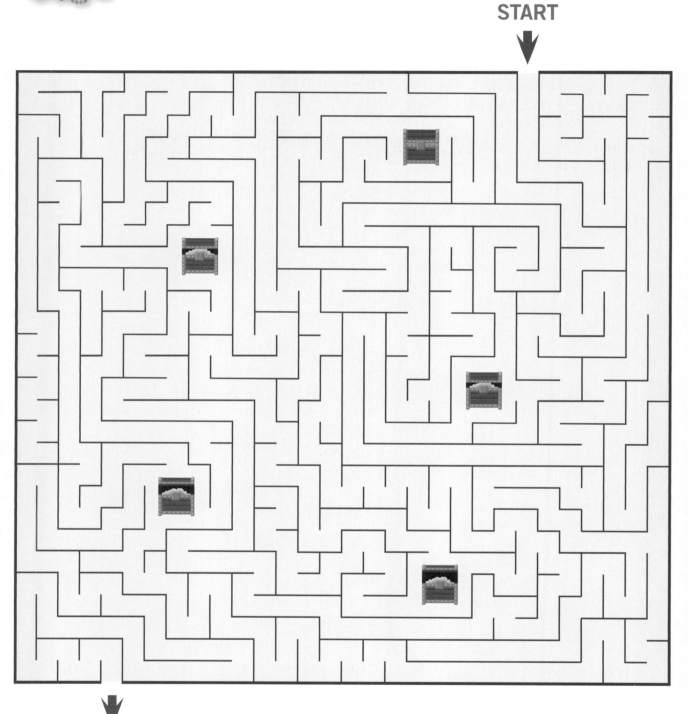

FINISH

FRIENDS IN NEED

Pretend the blue line is a mirror. Cross out letters on the top half of the grid that have incorrect mirror images on the bottom half. The remaining right-side-up letters will spell a way to keep a team Dungeons session going and going and going.

```
I M O R E V O E I V P E T E P L A
M M A T Y E R E S W H Y G H E N T
S H E U Y A R D E N E D O T W O N
─────────────────────────────────
E H E S Y A R R O C E D O K M S N
M M A T T H A E S M T I H E N T
C A W R E A I N I A C E T E M I A
```

___ ___ ___ ___ ___ ___   ___ ___ ___ ___ ___ ___ ___ ___

___ ___ ___ ___   ___ ___ ___   ___ ___ ___   ___ ___ ___ ___.

LOST IN PUMPKIN PASTURES

Can you get to the warning bell before skeletons get to you?

Begin in the gold start square. Move in the direction an arrow points until you come to a new sign. If there are two arrows in a square, you can choose to go either direction. Can you find the path that leads to the bell without running into a hostile mob?

START

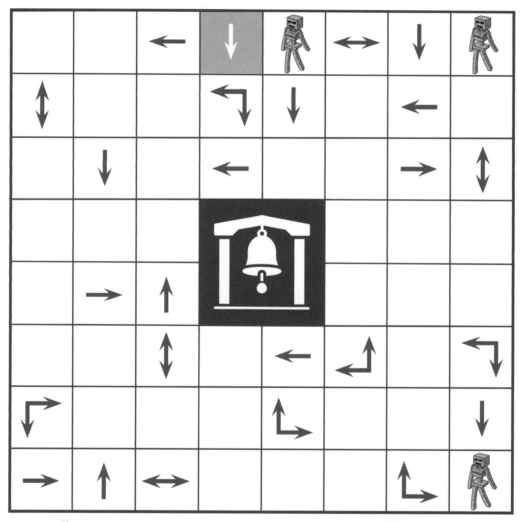

PINPOINT THE PIG

There's a **piggy bank** here somewhere. It appears only once in the letters below, forward or backward, in a horizontal, vertical, or diagonal line. Can you find and circle it before it gets away?

G I P K A B Y G G I P G

N N P I N K A P I N K A

A B A N K A B Y G G I P

B K P B I G B P I G A I

Y P N G Y B A N K P B G

G I G A P G P Y I N Y B

G G P B B A I G K G G Y

I G N A B Y G P I P G B

P Y G N I Y G G G A I A

I B K K B N I G B I P N

N A N A I P I G I A P K

Y N A B Y G G I B P N A

REPLAY BENEFITS

Start at the ↓. Write every third letter on the spaces until all the letters have been used. If you place them correctly, you'll discover a reason to replay different levels in Minecraft Dungeons.

↓

S I E R O A E N R P S U E T P A O G T E R M A A I R D S N E S G S

R ___ ___ ___ ___ ___ ___   ___ ___ ___ ___ ___   ___ ___

___ ___ ___ ___   ___ ___ ___ ___ ___   ___ ___ ___ ___ ___ ___ ___ ___ ___ .

UNLOCK THE RUNE

One of these 9 buttons is magic. If you press it first, you will touch each button only once, finish on F (final), and unlock the rune to take with you on your journey. You must follow the direction codes on the buttons.

For instance, 2D means press the button two spaces down. R = right. L = left. U = up.

Circle the magic button.

WHAT'S THE MEANING OF THIS?

Match each puzzle piece to its correct spot on the grid (piece A-1 belongs in row A, column 1), and shade the grid squares to match. When you're finished, you'll reveal the term for a Minecraft build that's easy to destroy.

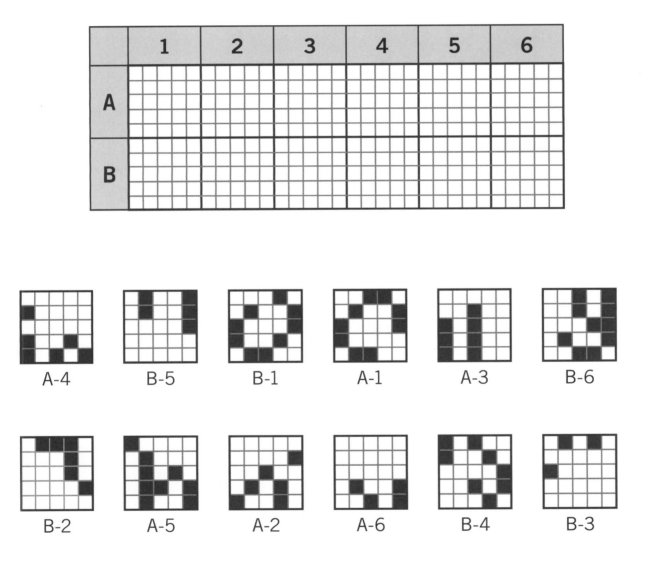

PERFECT PARAPHERNALIA

Read the writing on the wall by placing the 2x2 letter blocks in their proper places. If you place them correctly, you'll reveal a Minecraft Dungeons tip. Heads up: Words are separated by solid green squares and wrap from one line to the next.

S	E	E		T	H	E		W
R	I	T	I	N	G		O	N
	T	H	E		W	A	L	L

Grid:

C			A	T	E			Y
O				I	D			
L		G			R			
		H			N	C		H
		T	M	E	N	T		S

Letter blocks:

I	T
A	N

E	A
	E

R	E
U	R

E	A
	W

UNIQUE ABILITIES

Begin at the dot below each weapon and follow the line downward. Every time you hit a horizontal line (one that goes across), you must take it. If you follow the lines correctly, you'll know which weapons provide which effects.

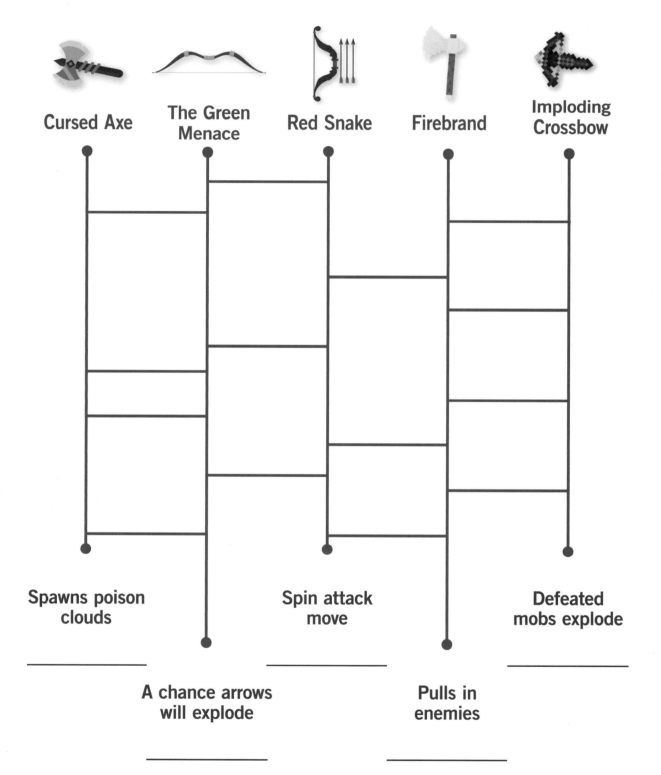

Cursed Axe

The Green Menace

Red Snake

Firebrand

Imploding Crossbow

Spawns poison clouds

Spin attack move

Defeated mobs explode

_____

A chance arrows will explode

Pulls in enemies

_____

_____

ARMOR QUEST

Different kinds of armor offer different protection in Minecraft Dungeons, and some armor drops more often than others. Can you find the twelve different kinds of unique armor in the word search below? If you find them all, the remaining letters reveal a tip for choosing armor.

Circle individual letters instead of whole words so you can see the leftover letters more easily.

M	L	A	T	C	H	Y	R	O	T
U	R	A	R	C	H	E	R	S	R
C	A	R	T	S	N	E	H	M	A
E	U	O	O	E	H	R	I	T	W
V	O	R	G	T	M	F	G	Y	L
I	E	A	I	F	R	L	H	O	A
H	D	W	U	O	R	F	L	I	T
E	G	H	S	X	U	T	A	U	S
E	I	T	N	G	S	S	N	T	F
B	Y	L	E	ⓢ	ⓟ	ⓘ	ⓓ	ⓔ	ⓡ

ARCHER'S

BEEHIVE

CURIOUS

FOX

FROST

FULL METAL

HERO'S

HIGHLAND

RENEGADE

~~SPIDER~~

STALWART

WITHER

Unused letters:

__ __ __ __ __ __ __ __ __ __ __ __ __ __ __ __ __

__ __ __ __ __ __ __ __ __ __ __ __ __ __ __ __ .

MIND. BLOWN.

Every word in Column B contains the same letters as a word in Column A, plus one letter. Draw a line between each word in Column A and its partner in Column B, then write the extra letter on the space provided. Read the column of letters downward to reveal the name of a useful artifact. The first one has been done for you.

COLUMN A	COLUMN B	
Road	Power	**W**
Soft	Items	__
Rope	Enter	__
Gist	Sword	__
Rows	Hoard	__
Stem	Route	__
True	Frost	__
Tree	Sting	__

__ __ __ __   __ __ __ __

MAZMORRAS, KERKER, DONJONS

The four players listed below are playing in four different languages.

Use the clues to find out which player is using which language. Put an X in a box if it can be ruled out. Put an O in boxes that are a match.

		LANGUAGE			
		English	German	Korean	Spanish
PLAYER	A				
	B				
	C				
	D				

1. A is not playing in English, Korean, or Spanish.

2. B is not playing in German, and C is not playing in English or Korean.

3. If A is playing in German, then D is playing in English.

MYSTERY PUZZLE MERCHANT

Prove your puzzle skills and earn a mystery weapon, piece of armor, or artifact from a merchant. Follow the instructions.

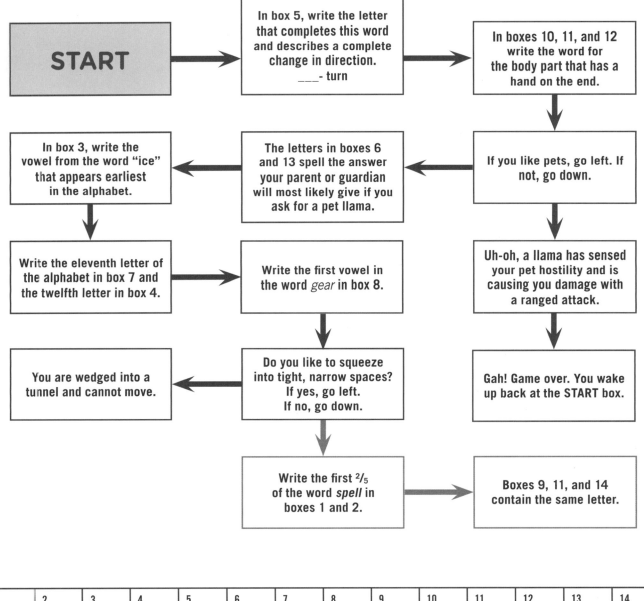

START

In box 5, write the letter that completes this word and describes a complete change in direction.
___- turn

In boxes 10, 11, and 12 write the word for the body part that has a hand on the end.

If you like pets, go left. If not, go down.

The letters in boxes 6 and 13 spell the answer your parent or guardian will most likely give if you ask for a pet llama.

In box 3, write the vowel from the word "ice" that appears earliest in the alphabet.

Write the eleventh letter of the alphabet in box 7 and the twelfth letter in box 4.

Write the first vowel in the word *gear* in box 8.

Uh-oh, a llama has sensed your pet hostility and is causing you damage with a ranged attack.

You are wedged into a tunnel and cannot move.

Do you like to squeeze into tight, narrow spaces? If yes, go left. If no, go down.

Gah! Game over. You wake up back at the START box.

Write the first ²/₅ of the word *spell* in boxes 1 and 2.

Boxes 9, 11, and 14 contain the same letter.

1	2	3	4	5	6	7	8	9	10	11	12	13	14

SNAG GEAR

Turn SNAG into GEAR one letter at a time. The answer to each clue looks like the word above it, except one letter is different. If you get stuck, try working from the bottom up.

S	N	A	G

An adult male deer

A point of light in the night sky, or a celebrity

To burn the surface of (often a steak, to seal in the juices)

G	E	A	R

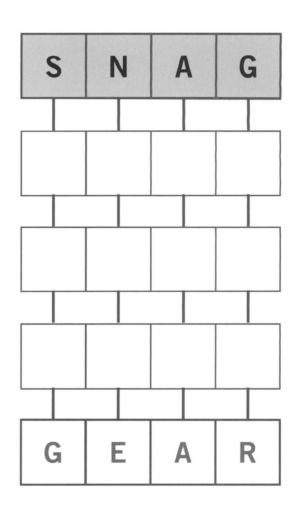

A STRING OF SUMMONS

Put your pencil point on the circled letter in the lower right corner of the grid. Without picking up the point, connect all the letters in the grid vertically or horizontally (not diagonally) to spell the names of the mobs you can summon for help when you're under attack. Write the name of the last mob in the blank space provided.

Example:

T	A	H	(S)
E	B	E	E
E	M	A	P
B	A	L	L

SHEEP
LLAMA
BEE
BAT

T	N	O	G	R	I
E	A	L	N	O	F
D	H	E	M	O	L
S	C	N	E	W	D
H	E	E	W	I	R
M	A	P	L	Z	A
A	L	L	U	O	(S)

SOUL WIZARD

WOLF

IRON GOLEM

ENCHANTED SHEEP

_____

NAVIGATION NIGHTMARE

Uh-oh. There are three exits but only one way out of this creepy Minecraft Dungeons cave. Can you find it without running into a cave spider?

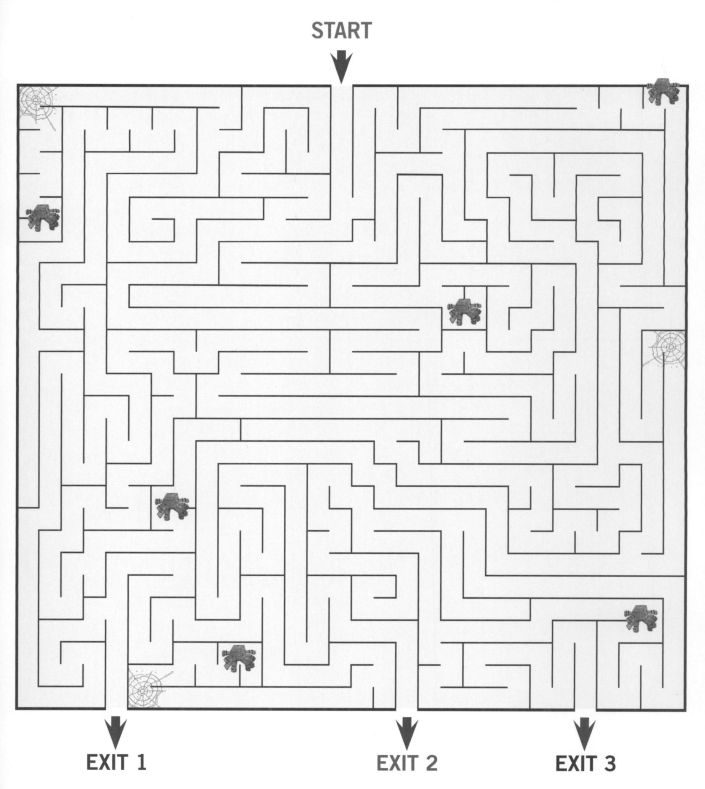

START

EXIT 1   EXIT 2   EXIT 3

XP FAST TRACK

Pretend the blue line is a mirror. Cross out letters on the top half of the grid that have incorrect mirror images on the bottom half. The remaining right-side-up letters will spell a way to get XP fast and level up.

C L E A N A M P A T S W A P A W G

U N I N E G B L O G A C K S T R O

K O W I S I L Y U L M O S F B O S

―――――――――――――――――――――――――――――――――

K E N I T G O I T W O U T B S S

H N I A C B G O U C K S T O M

C E A R M M P A T S E N P A M C

___ ___ ___ ___   ___ ___   ___ ___ ___ ___ ___ ___ ___ ___ ___

___ ___ ___ ___ ___ ___ ___   ___ ___ ___   ___ ___ ___ ___ ___ ___   ___ ___ ___ ___.

CRUSH THE CAULDRON

Your mission: avoid the witches and get to the Corrupted Cauldron to destroy it!

Begin in the orange square. Move in the direction an arrow points until you come to a new arrow. If there are two arrows in a square, you can choose to go either direction.

START

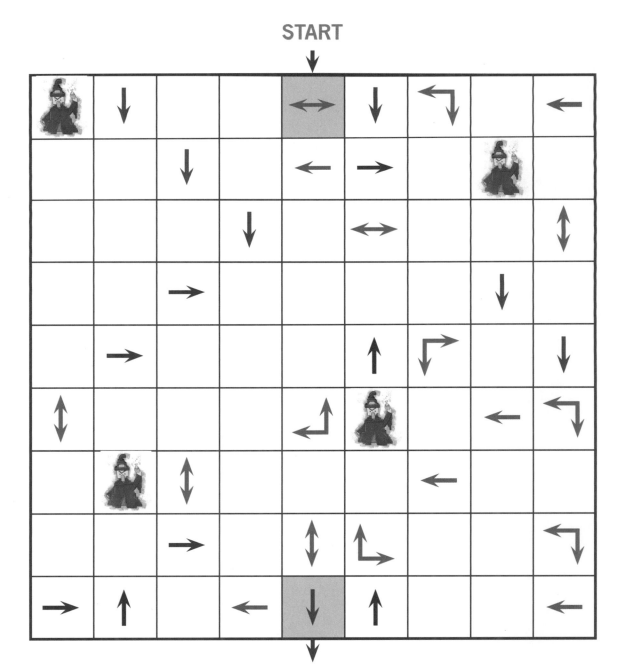

SECRET LEVEL

Minecraft Dungeons is full of secret locations. Can you find the **Creepy Crypt** in the word search of letters below? It appears only once, forward or backward, in a horizontal, vertical, or diagonal line.

```
Y  C  P  T  Y  R  C  Y  P  E  E  R  C
T  C  R  Y  P  T  T  R  Y  P  C  R  T
E  P  C  E  C  E  P  E  C  T  E  Y  P
R  T  Y  R  E  R  Y  C  R  E  R  R  R
T  P  Y  R  E  P  R  T  P  C  Y  C  Y
C  Y  C  T  C  E  C  Y  Y  Y  P  Y  C
C  R  E  E  P  Y  R  P  C  P  E  P  Y
T  C  E  C  T  Y  E  Y  T  E  E  E  P
R  Y  T  E  P  R  E  T  C  E  R  E  E
T  P  Y  R  C  Y  P  E  E  R  C  R  E
P  E  E  R  Y  P  Y  P  E  C  Y  C  R
C  R  E  E  P  Y  C  R  E  P  T  P  C
C  C  R  E  E  P  Y  C  R  Y  P  E  T
```

PETTY DRAMA

Some ways of defeating mobs are more entertaining than others. Decipher this code to reveal a fun one.

Start at the ↓. Write every third letter on the spaces until all have been used. If you place them correctly, you'll reveal a tip for destroying mobs.

0

___ ___ ___ ___ ___ ___ ___ ___ ___   ___ ___ ___ ___ ___ ___ ___   ___ ___ ___ ___

___ ___ ___ ___ ___ ___ ___ ___ ___   ___ ___ ___ ___ ___ ___ ___ ___   ___ ___ ___ ___.

UNLOCK THE RUNE

One of these 25 buttons is magic. If you press it first, you will touch each button only once, finish on F (final), and unlock the rune to take with you on your journey.

2D means press the button two spaces down. R = right. L = left. U = up.

Circle the magic button.

4D	4D	1R	1R	2D
1R	1U	2R	F	3D
2U	1L	1U	1L	3L
2U	2R	1D	1U	2L
3R	1U	4U	3U	1U

BIGGER, STRONGER, FASTER

Gaming has its own language. Build a gaming term from the blocks below.

Match each puzzle piece to its correct spot on the grid (piece A-1 belongs in row A, column 1), and shade the grid squares to match. When you're finished, you'll reveal the name of a gaming term for an increase of power.

	1	2	3	4	5	6
A						
B						

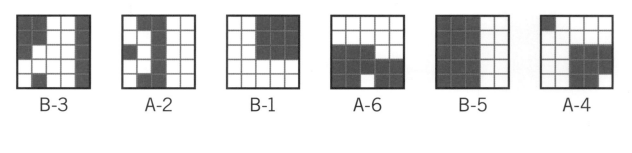

B-3 A-2 B-1 A-6 B-5 A-4

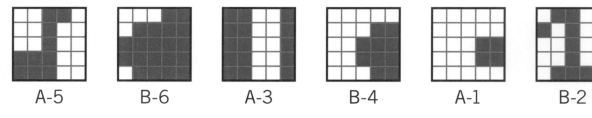

A-5 B-6 A-3 B-4 A-1 B-2

POWER POCKETS

Read the writing on the wall by placing the 2x2 letter blocks in their proper places. If you place them correctly, you'll reveal a fact that will help you build the most powerful equipment. Heads up: Words are separated by solid blue squares and wrap from one line to the next.

S	E	E		T	H	E		W
R	I	T	I	N	G		O	N
	T	H	E		W	A	L	L

G			R		W			H
			R	E	E			N
C	H	A			M	E	N	T
	S	L			S			
	R			E		A		
	P			E	R	F	U	L

A	R
O	W

N	T
O	T

E	A
T	H

I	T
	E

I	S
N	D

BRILLIANT BUILDS

Follow the trails below to reveal four Minecraft Dungeons gear combinations, also known as builds.

Begin at the dot below each weapon and follow the trail downward to the armor and then to the artifact. Every time you hit a horizontal trail (one that goes across), you must take it.

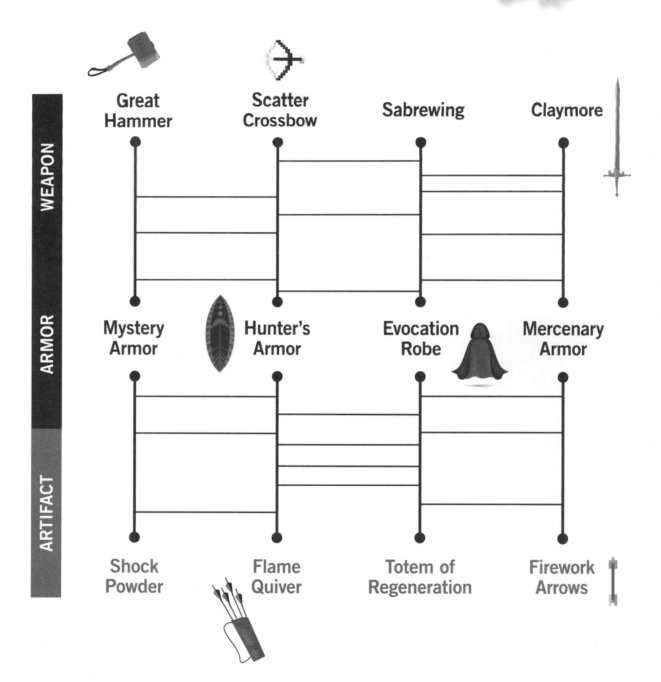

WEAPON

Great Hammer   Scatter Crossbow   Sabrewing   Claymore

ARMOR

Mystery Armor   Hunter's Armor   Evocation Robe   Mercenary Armor

ARTIFACT

Shock Powder   Flame Quiver   Totem of Regeneration   Firework Arrows

LOCATION LOCATION

Hidden in the word search below are the missing halves of the 14 location names in Minecraft Dungeons. Unscramble the letters to figure out the word you need to find. If you find them all, the remaining letters reveal a suggestion for finding your way through these locations in the game.

Hint: Circle individual letters instead of whole words so you can see the leftover letters more easily.

E	Y	R	E	I	F	E	S	X	K
L	P	L	O	R	T	Q	E	T	C
P	O	E	U	R	U	C	N	L	O
M	A	O	N	I	E	C	A	B	L
E	K	(S)	(D)	(O)	(O)	(W)	S	C	B
T	C	S	T	H	T	I	O	Y	H
E	A	R	A	U	D	S	G	L	G
C	V	V	Y	I	R	G	D	R	I
E	E	T	A	P	O	E	A	E	H
N	R	N	E	S	T	A	S	S	R

___ COAST	(DISQU)
~~SECRET ___~~	~~(OWOSD)~~
CREEPY ___	(RCTPY)
___ SWAMP	(GOSGY)
SOGGY ___	(AVEC)
PUMPKIN ___	(STRAPSUE)
ARCH ___	(VEHAN)
___ CANYON	(TACCI)
___ MINES	(NOTDEERS)
DESERT ___	(PLETEM)
___ TEMPLE	(ORWEL)
___ FORGE	(REIFY)
___ HALLS	(GLOBCHIKH)
___ PINNACLE	(DOBISANI)

Unused letters:

___ ___ ___ ___ ___ ___ ___   ___ ___   ___ ___ ___ ___ ___ ___

___ ___ ___ ___ ___ ___   ___ ___ ___ ___ ___ .

IRON FIST

Every word in Column B contains the same letters as a word in Column A, plus one letter. Draw a line between each word in Column A and its partner in Column B, then write the extra letter on the space provided. Unscramble the letters to reveal an artifact that can summon extra protection.

COLUMN A	COLUMN B	
Undone	Sellers	L
Scenes	Stories	__
Unreal	Erratic	__
Lesser	Emerald	__
Crater	Dungeon	__
Stared	Neutral	__
Resist	Darkest	__
Leader	Essence	__

__ __ __ __ __   __ __ __

REAP A SOUL

Turn REAP into SOUL one letter at a time. The answer to each clue looks like the word above it, except one letter is different. If you get stuck, try working from the bottom up.

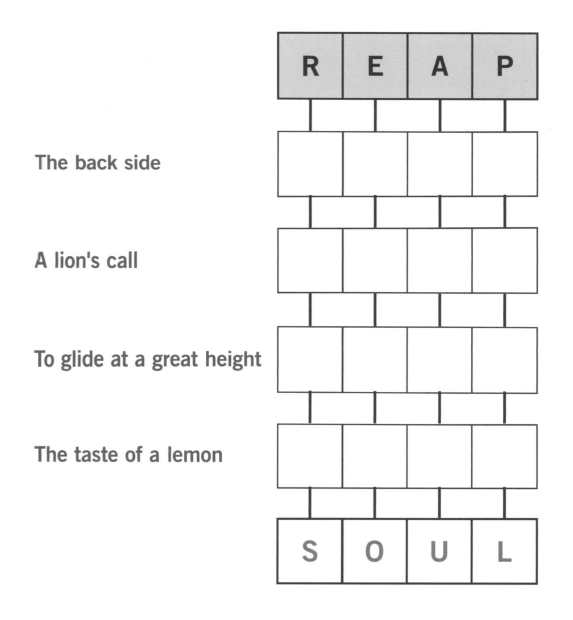

| R | E | A | P |

The back side

A lion's call

To glide at a great height

The taste of a lemon

| S | O | U | L |

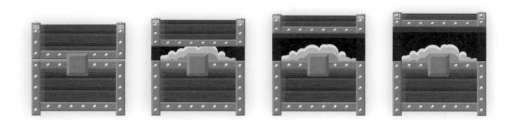

A STRING OF UNDEAD MOBS

Put your pencil point on the circled letter in the grid. Without picking up the point, connect all the letters in the grid vertically or horizontally (not diagonally) to spell the names of six undead mobs. The first four are provided for you. Fill in the names of the last two undead mobs as you go!

Example:

T	A	H	Ⓢ
F	B	E	E
E	M	A	P
B	A	L	L

SHEEP
LLAMA
BEE
BAT

Y	Z	E	H	P	N	A	M	E
B	O	I	A	N	H	O	R	S
A	M	B	N	O	T	E	K	Ⓢ
B	H	T	T	O	E	L	N	C
R	A	I	N	M	O	M	A	E
W	K	C	E	C	R	C	I	R
Y	E	O	J	N	E	K	H	C

SKELETON HORSEMAN

PHANTOM

NECROMANCER

CHICKEN JOCKEY

_____

_____

UNDER A SPELL

You have just arrived at Arch Haven on a ship.
Complete the maze by collecting four spell books and
getting back to the ship.

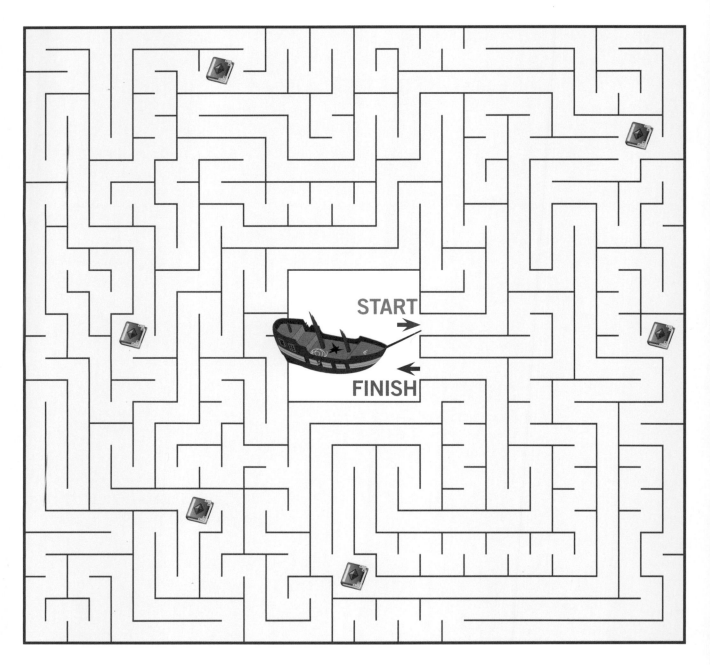

PLAYER BEWARE

Pretend the blue line is a mirror. Cross out letters on the top half of the grid that have incorrect mirror images on the bottom half. Write the remaining letters from the top half on the spaces to reveal a Minecraft Dungeons word of warning.

```
A M C O O B S O S T I K I L E L A
T T W A C O U K W H L E N Y O D U
B E R M A Y U P I M S O M P E Y N
```

———————————————————————————

```
Я S Я W E Λ P I E O Я E E N
T T A C N D K W H P E N Λ O E N
B W E Λ O B S Г S T I E R T Г Λ
```

___ ___ ___ ___   ___ ___ ___ ___   ___ ___ ___   ___ ___ ___ ___ ___

___ ___ ___ ___ ___   ___ ___ ___   ___ ___ ___ ___ .

46

TO THE TEMPLE

This wacky map marks the way to the temple. As you proceed, power the beacon to reveal the rest of the way.

From Start, move in the direction an arrow points until you come to a new arrow. If there are two arrows in a square, you can choose to go either direction.

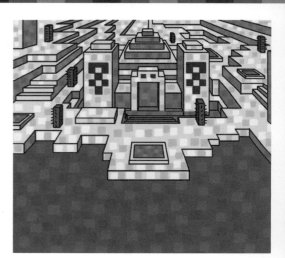

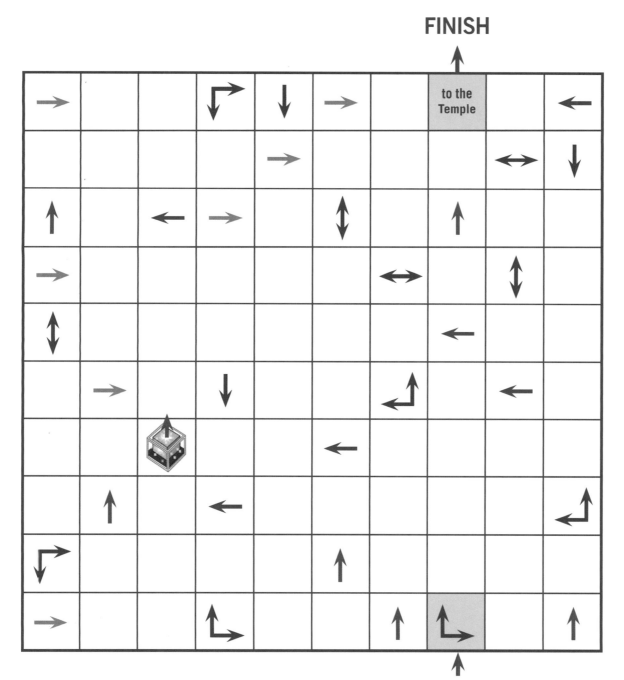

FINISH

START

CLASSIC WEAPON

*It's a classic! Can you find the **diamond sword** in this apocalyptic word search? It appears only once, forward or backward, in a horizontal, vertical, or diagonal line.*

```
D I S D R O W S D N O M I A D
R A W S I N D I R M I A D R I
W M O D I A M N O D S W O M A
S S R N M S M D W A D W I W M
D O D S D O I O S W S A S D R
N M D N N W N N D D I D M N O
O A N D O M O D N S N A I O W
M I O S W M S M O O W M N M S
A D M O M D A I M S A O D A D
I I A A N I M D A O D M R I N
D N I S D N O W I A N S N D O
M D D I A M O N D S W R O D M
A N O O A S W O R O D I A N A
I R W I R A I D R O W S W I I
D S D I M O N D S W O R D A D
```

RACK 'EM UP

There's nothing worse than running out of resources during a battle. Use this tip to stay well stocked.

Start at the ↓. Write every third letter on the spaces until all have been used. If you place them correctly, you'll reveal a tip to rack up essential resources.

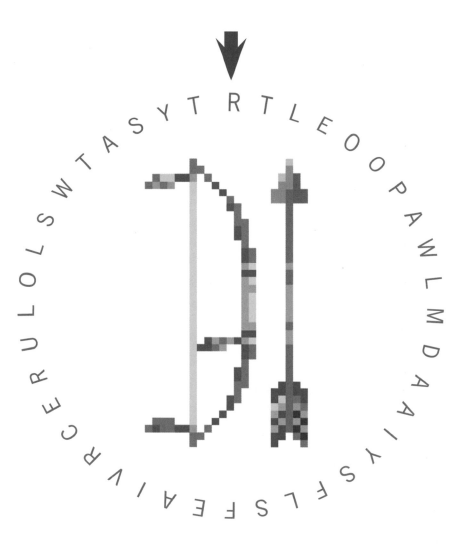

R ___ ___ ___ ___ ___ ___   ___ ___ ___ ___ ___ ___

___ ___   ___ ___ ___   ___ ___ ___ ___ ___ ___ ___

___ ___   ___ ___ ___ ___ ___ ___   ___ ___ ___ ___ ___ ___ .

UNLOCK THE RUNE

One of these 36 buttons is magic. If you press it first, you will touch each button only once, finish on F (final), and unlock the rune to take with you on your journey.

2D means press the button two spaces down.
R = right. L = left. U = up. Circle the magic button.

Hint: Start at the F button and work backwards if that helps.

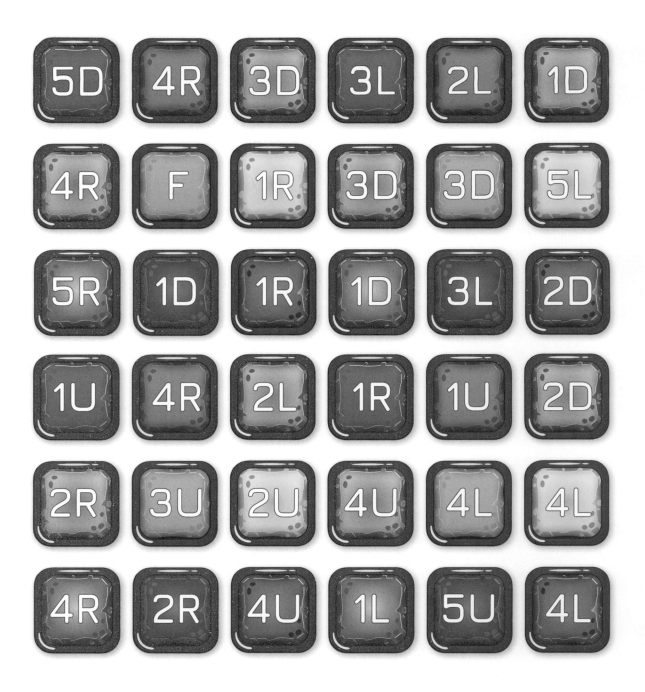

BOSS BATTLE WARNING

Read the writing on the wall by placing the 2x2 letter blocks in their proper places. If you place them correctly, you'll reveal a flaw in one boss battle strategy. Don't make this mistake! Heads up: Words are separated by blue squares and wrap from one line to the next.

S	E	E		T	H	E		W
R	I	T	I	N	G		O	N
	T	H	E		W	A	L	L

A				U	L		F
U	E					B	U
I	L	D				Y	
L			E		P		
E			A	N	D		
A	I	L				A	I
N						S	I
N			E		F	O	E

A	G
A	

D	
M	A

S	O
L	E

O	W
	F

O	S
R	

S	T
G	L

COUCH CO-OP

Four friends have teamed up to play Minecraft Dungeons together online. Follow the trails to identify how each player is outfitted.

Begin at the dot below each name and follow the trail downward. Every time you hit a horizontal trail (one that goes across), you must take it.

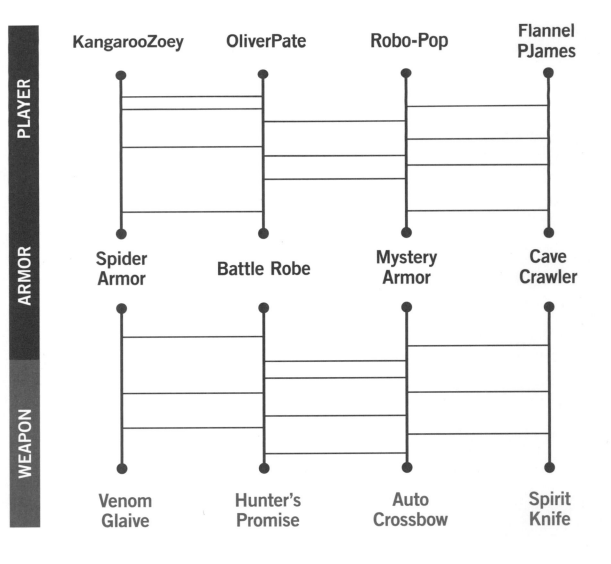

PLAYER

KangarooZoey   OliverPate   Robo-Pop   Flannel PJames

ARMOR

Spider Armor   Battle Robe   Mystery Armor   Cave Crawler

WEAPON

Venom Glaive   Hunter's Promise   Auto Crossbow   Spirit Knife

ENCHANTMENT ENHANCEMENT

Boost the power of weapons and armor with enchantments. Can you find the 17 different enchantments in the word search below? If you find them all, the remaining letters reveal a tip for getting surprising results from enchantments.

Hint: Circle individual letters instead of whole words so you can see leftover letters more easily.

T	E	M	P	O	T	H	E	F	T	R	
T	O	H	S	E	C	N	A	I	D	A	R
M	Y	E	O	D	A	C	R	O	B	A	T
U	H	E	C	H	O	E	D	B	C	O	G
L	C	G	N	I	T	N	A	H	C	N	U
T	N	H	M	R	D	R	B	O	I	S	Y
I	U	F	A	O	R	R	R	G	U	N	T
S	P	I	I	I	O	M	A	N	Y	D	I
H	L	Q	E	U	N	P	O	W	E	R	V
O	E	R	S	K	M	S	I	L	O	L	A
T	I	H	L	A	C	I	T	I	R	C	R
A	L	T	R	U	I	S	T	I	C	S	G

ACROBAT
ALTRUISTIC
BARRIER
CHAINS
COWARDICE
CRITICAL HIT
DYNAMO
ECHO
FIRE TRAIL
GRAVITY
MULTISHOT
POWER
PUNCH
RADIANCE SHOT
RAMPAGING
~~TEMPO THEFT~~
UNCHANTING

Unused letters:

__ __ __   __ __ __   __ __ __ __ __ __ __ __

__ __ __   __ __ __ __ __ __   __ __ __ __ __ __ __ .

A GATHERING STORM

Every word in Column B contains the same letters as a word in Column A, plus one letter. Draw a line between each word in Column A and its partner in Column B, then write the extra letter on the space provided. Unscramble the letters to reveal an explosive artifact. The first one has been done for you.

COLUMN A	COLUMN B	
Reply	Escape	**S**
Crest	Glaive	__
Racer	Desert	__
Peace	Record	__
Curse	Player	__
Coder	Trader	__
Agile	Secret	__
Reeds	Rescue	__
Rated	Archer	__

__ __ __ __ __ __ __ __ __

ROLL TO LEAP

Turn ROLL into LEAP one letter at a time. The answer to each clue looks like the word above it, except one letter is different. If you get stuck, try working from the bottom up.

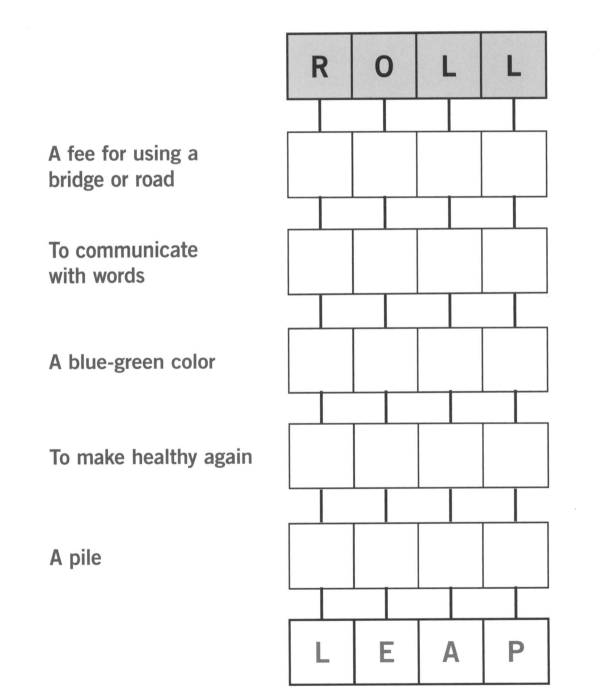

| R | O | L | L |

A fee for using a bridge or road

To communicate with words

A blue-green color

To make healthy again

A pile

| L | E | A | P |

A STRING OF BOSS MOBS

Put your pencil point on the circled letter in the grid. Without picking up the point, connect all the letters in the grid vertically or horizontally (not diagonally) to spell the names of the six boss mobs in this attack. Fill in the names of the last two mobs in the spaces provided.

Example:

T	A	H	Ⓢ
E	B	E	E
E	M	A	P
B	A	L	L

SHEEP
LLAMA
BEE
BAT

O	N	H	E	A	R	T	R	M	O
R	C	D	E	T	P	O	E	D	O
D	A	E	M	O	U	F	E	N	S
L	U	N	O	N	R	R	O	R	H
E	D	S	T	S	E	R	C	O	O
Ⓡ	S	O	R	T	G	T	S	N	M
T	I	I	L	L	A	R	O	O	M
Y	C	H	O	S	L	E	S	I	T
A	R	E	N	S	E	M	A	N	Y

REDSTONE MONSTROSITY

ARCH-ILLAGER

CORRUPTED CAULDRON

HEART OF ENDER

_____

_____

56

SECRET LEVEL: MOOSHROOM ATTACK

Avoid the mooshrooms and make it from start to finish through the secret cow level.

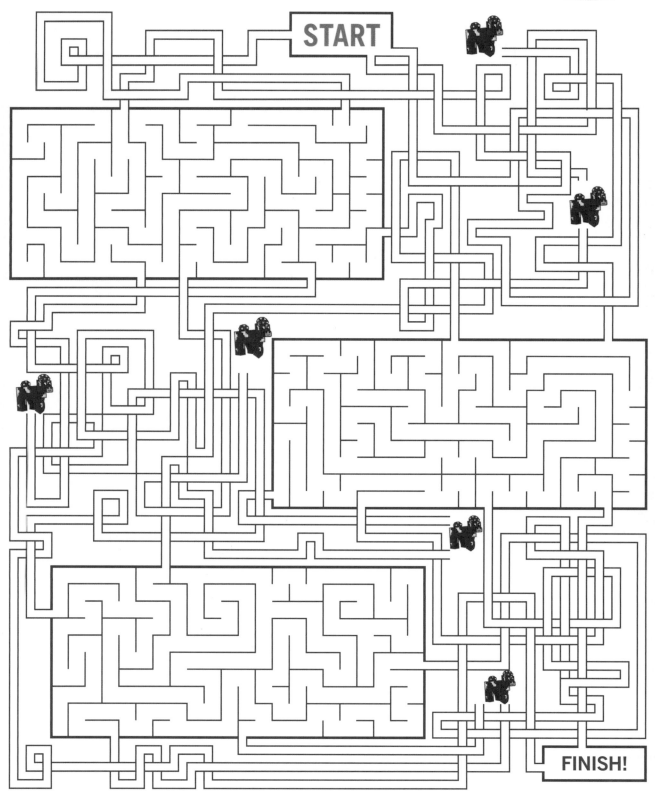

ANSWERS

THE HIDDEN CATACOMB page 4

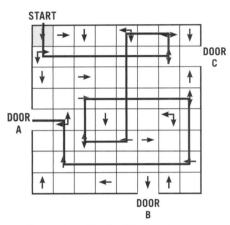

Door A is the hidden entrance to the catacomb.

LOST VILLAGER page 5

V V E G A L L I V G
G I I E V R G I I E
R L L L I L G L R
E L A L L L R E I
V I L L A E R E G L
L G V G L G G G G L
L E E I L A E A E A
I R V I L L V L R G
V I L L A G I I V E
R V I L L A G V E R

A HEALTHY DOSE OF ADVICE page 6

KILL COWS AND SHEEP FOR HEALTH REWARDS.

☾ UNLOCK THE RUNE page 7

2R	1L	2D
1R	1U	F
1U	1L	1U

HIDDEN ACRONYM page 8

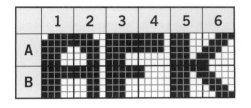

AFK stands for Away From Keyboard.

BATTLE BREAKS page 9

E	X	P	L	O	R	E			C	A
M	P		B	E	T	W	E	E	N
		L	E	V	E	L	S		T	O
	F	I	N	D		E	M	E	R
A	L	D		C	H	E	S	T	S

ON THE TRACK OF THE ARTIFACT page 10

Fireworks Arrow - Redstone Mine
Death Cap Mushroom - Highblock Halls
Buzzy Nest - Soggy Cave
Love Medallion - Panda Plateau
Ghost Cloak - Obsidian Pinnacle

CROSSBOW QUEST page 11

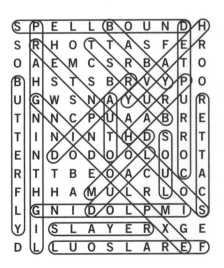

SHOTS FROM CROSSBOWS CANNOT BE CHARGED.

A FANTASTIC FIND page 12

COLUMN A	COLUMN B	
Tonic	Target	T
Nomad	Action	A
Cache	Spider	S
Ocean	Battle	T
Grand	Dynamo	Y
Great	Beacon	B
Table	Option	O
Point	Chance	N
Pride	Ranged	E

TASTY BONE

ARMORED AND DANGEROUS page 13

	BEENEST ARMOR	HIGHLAND ARMOR	EMBER ROBE
TAGURIT	X	O	X
POPSIZZLE11	O	X	X
COOOL28	X	X	O

ARCH-ILLAGER MAZE page 14

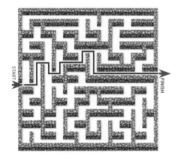

FIND LOOT
page 15

A STRING OF MOBS
page 16

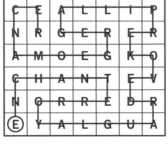

ENCHANTER
ROYAL GUARD
EVOKER
PILLAGER
GEOMANCER

SOGGY SWAMP MAZE page 17

FRIENDS IN NEED page 18

REVIVE TEAMMATES WHEN THEY ARE DOWN.

LOST IN PUMPKIN PASTURES page 19

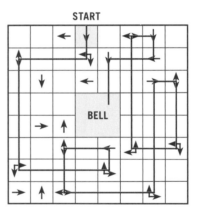

PINPOINT THE PIG page 20

```
G  I  P  K  A  B  Y  G  G  I  P  G
N  N  P  I  N  K  A  P  I  N  K  A
A  B  A  N  K  A  B  Y  G  G  I  P
B  K  P  B  I  G  B  P  I  G  A  I
Y  P  N  G  Y  B  A  N  K  P  B  G
G  I  G  A  P  G  P  Y  I  N  Y  B
G  G  P  B  B  A  I  G  K  G  G  Y
I  G  N  A  B  Y  G  P  I  P  G  B
P  Y  G  N  I  Y  G  G  A  I  A
I  B  K  K  B  N  I  G  B  I  P  N
N  A  N  A  I  P  I  G  I  A  P  K
Y  N  A  B  Y  G  G  I  B  P  N  A
```

REPLAY BENEFITS page 21

REPEAT MISSIONS TO EARN GEAR UPGRADES.

≈ UNLOCK THE RUNE page 22

2R	2D	3D	(2L)
1R	2D	1D	1L
2U	2R	2L	1U
2U	F	1R	3L

WHAT'S THE MEANING OF THIS?
page 23

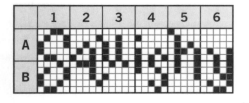

	1	2	3	4	5	6
A						
B						

SQUISHY *refers to a build that is easily damaged or killed. Sometimes a player will sacrifice durability for power or speed and choose a squishy build.*

PERFECT PARAPHERNALIA page 24

C	R	E	A	T	E	■	Y
O	U	R	■	I	D	E	A
L	■	G	E	A	R	■	W
I	T	H	■	E	N	C	H
A	N	T	M	E	N	T	S

UNIQUE ABILITIES page 25

Cursed Axe - Defeated mobs explode

The Green Menace - Spawns poison clouds

Red Snake - A chance arrows will explode

Firebrand - Spin attack move

Imploding Crossbow - Pulls in enemies

ARMOR QUEST page 26

MATCH YOUR ARMOR TO YOUR FIGHTING STYLE.

MIND. BLOWN. page 27

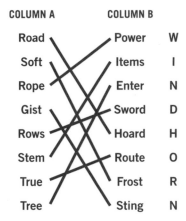

COLUMN A		COLUMN B	
Road		Power	W
Soft		Items	I
Rope		Enter	N
Gist		Sword	D
Rows		Hoard	H
Stem		Route	O
True		Frost	R
Tree		Sting	N

WIND HORN

MAZMORRAS, KERKER, DONJONS page 28
(These words mean "Dungeons" in Spanish, German, and French.)

	ENGLISH	GERMAN	KOREAN	SPANISH
A	X	O	X	X
B	X	X	O	X
C	X	X	X	O
D	O	X	X	X

MYSTERY PUZZLE MERCHANT
page 29

SPELUNKER ARMOR

SNAG GEAR page 30

S	N	A	G
S	T	A	G
S	T	A	R
S	E	A	R
G	E	A	R

A STRING OF SUMMONS page 31

SOUL WIZARD
WOLF
IRON GOLEM
ENCHANTED SHEEP
LLAMA

NAVIGATION NIGHTMARE page 32

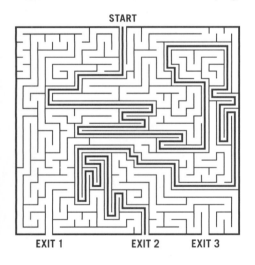

START

EXIT 1   EXIT 2   EXIT 3

XP FAST TRACK page 33

CAMP AT SPAWNING BLOCKS TO KILL MOBS.

CRUSH THE CAULDRON page 34

START

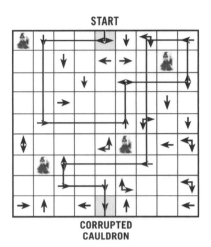

CORRUPTED
CAULDRON

SECRET LEVEL page 35

```
Y C P T Y R C Y P E E R C
T C R Y P T T R Y P C R T
E P C E C E P E C T E Y P
R T Y R E R Y C R E R R R
T P Y R E P R T P C Y C Y
C Y C T C E C Y Y Y P Y C
C R E E P Y R P C P E P Y
T C E C T Y E Y T E E E P
R Y T E P R E T C E R E E
T P Y R C Y P E E R C R E
P E E R Y P Y P E C Y C R
C R E E P Y C R E P T P C
C C R E E P Y C R Y P E T
```

PETTY DRAMA page 36

OVERWHELM ENEMIES WITH MULTIPLE
SUMMONED PETS.

△ UNLOCK THE RUNE page 37

4D	4D	1R	1R	2D
1R	1U	2R	F	3D
2U	1L	1U	1L	3L
2U	2R	1D	1U	2L
3R	1U	4U	3U	1U

BIGGER, STRONGER, FASTER page 38

	1	2	3	4	5	6
A						
B						

(Grid spelling "BUFF")

BUFF is an increase in the effect of an item.

POWER POCKETS page 39

G	E	A	R		W	I	T	H
	T	H	R	E	E		E	N
C	H	A	N	T	M	E	N	T
	S	L	O	T	S		I	S
	R	A	R	E		A	N	D
P	O	W	E	R	F	U	L	

BRILLIANT BUILDS page 40

WEAPON	ARMOR	ARTIFACT
Great Hammer	Hunter's Armor	Firework Arrows
Scatter Crossbow	Evocation Robe	Shock Powder
Sabrewing	Mystery Armor	Totem of Regeneration
Claymore	Mercenary Armor	Flame Quiver

LOCATION LOCATION page 41

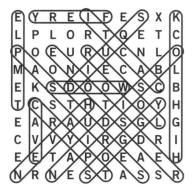

EXPLORE TO UNLOCK SECRET AREAS.

IRON FIST
page 42

COLUMN A	COLUMN B	
Undone	Sellers	L
Scenes	Stories	O
Unreal	Erratic	I
Lesser	Emerald	M
Crater	Dungeon	G
Stared	Neutral	T
Resist	Darkest	K
Leader	Essence	E

GOLEM KIT

A STRING OF UNDEAD MOBS page 44

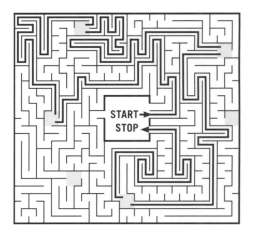

SKELETON HORSEMAN
PHANTOM
NECROMANCER
CHICKEN JOCKEY
WRAITH
BABY ZOMBIE

UNDER A SPELL page 45

(Maze with START → STOP)

PLAYER BEWARE page 46

MOBS STILL ATTACK WHEN YOUR MAP IS OPEN.

REAP A SOUL
page 43

R	E	A	P
R	E	A	R
R	O	A	R
S	O	A	R
S	O	U	R
S	O	U	L

TO THE TEMPLE page 47

CLASSIC WEAPON page 48

```
D I S D R O W S D N O M I A D
R A W S I N D I R M I A D R I
W M O D I A M N O D S W O M A
S S R N M S M D W A D W I W M
D O D S D O I O S W S A S D R
N M D N N W N N D D I D M N O
O A N D O M O D N S N A I O W
M I O S W M S M O O W M N M S
A D M O M D A I M S A O D A D
I I A A N I M D A O D M R I N
D N I S D N O W I A N S N D O
M D D I A M O N D S W R O D M
A N O O A S W O R O D I A N A
I R W I R A I D R O W S W I I
D S D I M O N D S W O R D A D
```

RACK 'EM UP page 49

REPLAY LEVELS AT LOW
DIFFICULTY TO AMASS ARROWS.

∞ UNLOCK THE RUNE page 50

5D	4R	3D	3L	2L	1D
4R	F	1R	3D	3D	5L
5R	1D	1R	1D	3L	2D
1U	4R	2L	1R	1U	2D
2R	3U	2U	4U	4L	4L
4R	2R	4U	1L	5U	4L

BOSS BATTLE WARNING page 51

A		S	O	U	L		F
U	E	L	E	D		B	U
I	L	D		M	A	Y	
L	O	S	E		P	O	W
E	R		A	N	D		F
A	I	L		A	G	A	I
N	S	T		A		S	I
N	G	L	E		F	O	E

COUCH CO-OP page 52

NAME	ARMOR	WEAPON
KangarooZoey	Mystery Armor	Venom Glaive
OliverPate	Spider Armor	Auto Crossbow
Robo-Pop	Cave Crawler	Hunter's Promise
Flannel PJames	Battle Robe	Spirit Knife

ENCHANTMENT ENHANCEMENT page 53

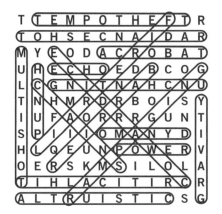

TRY ODD COMBOS FOR UNIQUE SKILLS.

A GATHERING STORM page 54

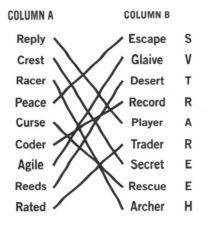

COLUMN A	COLUMN B	
Reply	Escape	S
Crest	Glaive	V
Racer	Desert	T
Peace	Record	R
Curse	Player	A
Coder	Trader	R
Agile	Secret	E
Reeds	Rescue	E
Rated	Archer	H

HARVESTER

ROLL TO LEAP page 55

R	O	L	L
T	O	L	L
T	E	L	L
T	E	A	L
H	E	A	L
H	E	A	P
L	E	A	P

A STRING OF BOSS MOBS page 56

O	N	H	E	A	R	T	R	M	O
R	C	D	E	T	P	O	E	D	O
D	A	E	M	O	U	F	E	N	S
L	U	N	O	N	R	R	O	R	H
E	D	S	T	S	E	R	C	O	O
ⓇR	S	O	R	T	G	T	S	N	M
T	I	L	L	A	R	O	O	M
Y	C	H	O	S	E	S	I	T
A	R	E	N	S	E	M	A	N	Y

SECRET LEVEL: MOOSHROOM ATTACK page 57

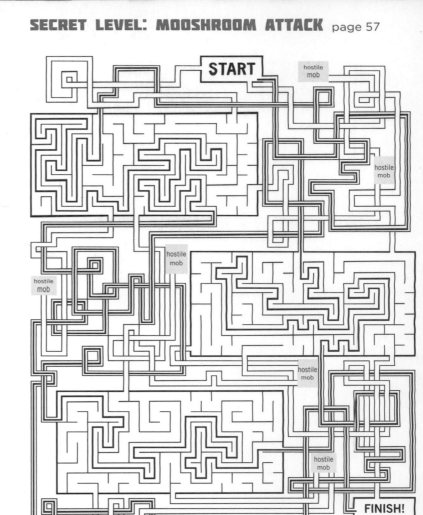

REDSTONE MONSTROSITY

ARCH-ILLAGER

CORRUPTED CAULDRON

HEART OF ENDER

MOOSHROOM MONSTROSITY

NAMELESS ONE